G000268977

Put on your walkin
in the knapsack . .
A fascinating jou
woods that surround an old Sussex village
Doris Hall, and you will find her a charming and wise
companion.

She grew up in this countryside beneath the lofty rolling
Downs. Her intimate knowledge of the wildlife, buildings
and history you will discover along the way are a source of
delight.

Find out why you must ask the elder tree's permission
before picking its flowers or berries . . . survey the patchwork of the Weald from the spot where a local clergyman
met his untimely end . . . get to know the various ghosts
that haunt an old mansion.

This is more than a book about a rural stroll. Doris Hall
has created a living map with her eye for vivid detail; the
journey rich in both atmosphere and anecdote.

It will appeal to anyone who loves England's heritage
and countryside – and you can savour it all without leaving
the comfort of your armchair.

★　★　★

Doris Hall is a Sussex woman through and through,
with an ancestry that has lived in the county since, as she
says, "the days of woad!" She was born and brought up in
Ditchling, the centrepiece of Dawn to Dawn, and is proud
of the fact that she has always lived within walking distance
of the picturesque old village.

Walking is one of her main interests and she was for
many years in great demand as a leader of walks because
her knowledge of local history made them so interesting.

She followed her father into the horticulture business and
this has helped to make her an authority on plants, their
beauties and uses.

She took to writing in 1980 when she published a book
on the hamlet of Westmeston, its history and characters.
This was followed in 1985 by Growing Up in Ditchling, an
account of her formative years in the place she loves so
well.

Doris Hall is in great demand as a speaker to Sussex
groups and organisations, and has been a regular contri-
butor to local radio.

Married with two children and two grandchildren, she
now lives at Westmeston.

Also by Doris Hall
Westmeston Sunrise, 1980
Growing up in Ditchling, 1985

A Stroll Around Ditchling
Dawn to Dawn

Doris M. Hall

Temple House Books
Sussex England

Temple House Books
25 High Street,
Lewes, Sussex
First published 1987
© Doris Hall 1987
Set in Linotron Bembo
Typeset by CST, Eastbourne
Printed in Great Britain by
Antony Rowe Ltd
Chippenham, Wilts

ISBN 0 86332 259 X

FOREWORD

In *A Stroll Around Ditchling – Dawn to Dawn,* Doris Hall takes the reader on a delightful country walk over the fields and through the woods between Ditchling and Westmeston. We learn the history of this beautiful part of Sussex, the birds and wild animals who share it with us and the people who lived their lives here.

Doris Hall was born in Ditchling and knows her home ground better than anyone. In *Dawn to Dawn* she creates a microcosm of the English countryside which brings it vividly to life. Decades of experience and observation have gone into this charming book and the reader will be the richer for having accompanied Doris Hall on this inspiring country walk.

Raymond Briggs 16 July 1986

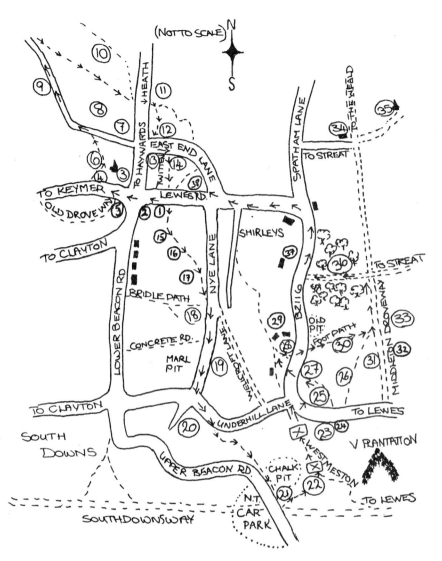

(NOT TO SCALE)

1. Village Hall, Ditchling
2. Frank Brangwyn's House
3. Ditchling Church
4. Old Well Site
5. Wing's Place
6. Village Green and Pond
7. Bowling Green
8. Lodge Hill
9. Viewing point to the west
10. Ditchling Court Gardens
11. Dumbrall's Estate
12. Friends' Meeting House
13. Old Post Office and Dymocks Manor
14. Unitarian Chapel
15. Browne Burial Plot
16. Lexden
17. Gospel Fields
18. Nye Wood
19. Vineyard
20. Gladstone's Head
21. Stile from which to view the Weald
22. Site of old Lime Burning Kilns
23. New Farm House, Westmeston
24. Site of Old Well
25. Lychgate and Westmeston Church
26. Old Rectory
27. Church Cottage
28. Westmeston Place
29. The Old Barn
30. Old Fairfield
31. Old Middleton House
32. Site of old Carpenter's Shop
33. New Middleton House
34. Hayleigh Farm
35. Streat Church/Streat Place
36. Sedlow Wood
37. Black Dog House
38. St Margaret's School, Ditchling

Dawn to Dawn

THERE is that period of time, between the passing of the night and the coming of the new day, just as the darkness of the night sky lightens to grey, as the stars cease to twinkle; this period is the dawn.

It is then that can be clearly heard the waters of the brook as it whispers its way over gravelly stones, that lay in its path as it wends its way – snake like – through meadows and woods, to join with the waters of countless other brooks that flow onwards to the sea. It is in this period that the pale primroses, soft cream in colour, and the shy violets, with either blue or white flowers, that grow with their roots nestling between clumps of ferns and moss – that also grow along the banks on each side of the brook – open their petals to emit a fragrance that is sweeter then than at any other time; it is as if the gentle dew has washed away all of the unpure odours that prevail in the daytime.

There are also the celandines which have no scent and are compensated for its lack by the brilliance of their colour. They never unfold their petals until the sun has gently kissed them, they then unfold as golden stars, like stars that at night time glow in the sky above and then with the coming of the new day have fallen to earth. A pair of water voles creep from their nest, one that they have so skil-

The Primrose

fully made near to the water's edge, but well hidden in the tangle of the roots of the alder, whose branches almost sweep the stones at the water's bottom. The voles daintily dip a paw each into the cool water and with this they wash away all traces of sleep from their eyes, before going to forage amongst the water weeds for themselves and their progeny.

The water rats awake, and watch, beady eyes alert for unguarded nests from which they hope to snatch an egg for their breakfast. The fronds of the ferns start to slowly unfurl, and as they do so make a tracery of patterns in the water below. Unhappily, almost before one has time to discern them, these patterns are distorted by the movement of the water and one is left to wonder if the pattern was just an illusion.

As the colour of the sky changes from grey to a pale orange, the voice of the nightingale is joined in song by the voices of the blackbird and then the song thrush, the perky little robin joins them. The sparrows twitter and the blue-grey doves softly coo. The bass of this choir of nature is supplied by the raucous cawing of the rooks and the crows.

A squirrel thus musically awakened sits outside its drey, head cocked to one side, as if listening to some great orchestral concert before leaping with agility from one branch of a tree to

The Badger   A Fox Cub

S. M. Hall

another until he reaches the ground, and he also on reaching the side of the brook performs his toilet, as is his nature.

A rabbit emerges from the bowels of the earth and starts to nibble the dew soaked herbage, for eating first, then making his toilet is a rabbit's habit.

A fox, wending his way homeward from a night of stealthy prowling, his brush held high, his hunger apparently satisfied on some unwary fowl, he ignores the rabbit, but marks the spot for a meal in the future.

Brock the badger, another nocturnal scavenger, makes his way homewards to sleep the day away in his earthy lair. After first cleaning the lair, for brock is a clean animal, unlike the fox, who lives amongst the bones of his prey.

A hare, seeing another of his kind, emits a warning. This ignored, he takes up the boxing stance of humans – who had it first, hare or human? – and the two joust for the rights of that secluded territory and the female hares that go with it. Some naturalist say that this jousting is the female rejecting the male's advances, I wonder who is right! The mist of the night sky clears from the sun, letting through a little promise of the warmth to come as the day grows older, the sky loses its orange glow and takes on a blueish tint.

The leaves on the trees start to unfurl, each showing as they

The Hare

S. M. Hall

do so their own distinctive shapes, and all sway as a very light breeze slightly ruffles them, as if the wind also is just awakening.

The deep purple flowers of the ash trees – which come out before the leaves – glisten as the sun shines on the dewdrop nestling in each slightly opened bud.

The lowing of the herd intermingling with the 'Gid up there' of the herdsman, wafts across the meadow as the cows make their way through dew soaked grass towards the milking parlour.

These calls are joined by the sound of a dog barking, as released from sleep he runs calling under the gradual lightening of the sky.

The *korr-korr* of the pheasant and the crowing of the cockerel as they awake and stretch adding their voices to the awakening sounds, it is as if they would tell the world 'get up, Dawn is here and it is time to start a new day.'

Stroll around Ditchling

SO thus having been awakened to the promise of a fine day, pack a day's rations in a rucksack or pocket; put on your most comfortable boots and come with me for a day's stroll.

Meet me at the car park that is to the rear of Ditchling Village Hall, for this being near to the crossroads is easy to find. We will commence our stroll from there.

No stroll should be hurried, and it should be interesting, so bear with me and I will describe each place we come to as we stroll along. A house was knocked down to make way for this car park, this was last used as a meeting place for the 1st Ditchling Scout Group.

The house had been converted from the classrooms, which were part of a school for boys, run by Mr Branfoot and his sister. This school was extensively damaged by fire in 1919 while the boys were away for the Easter holidays. Mr Branfoot retired and the site was sold. The buyer after converting the classrooms, moved into them. The fire damaged portion – nearest to the Lewes Road – remained derelict for some time, until enough money had been raised by public subscription to purchase and convert the old dormitories into Ditchling Village Hall. The sum of money needed was estimated at £1,000 of which £947.1.9d was donated by the residents of Ditchling, Westmeston and Streat. Concerts were held, also jumble sales, but a further £52.18.3d was needed, so a shilling fund was started with collecting boxes being placed in the various shops so that even those of limited means could contribute.

The rest of the house was completely demolished and a smaller house built, which stood where the exit from the car park is now. In the 1970s the hall was enlarged, it still incorporates part of the original building. We will now leave the car park and turning to the left pass Glynn's car show rooms; difficult now to imagine that this was once the drying ground of a hand laundry.

It was in a shed at the western side of the garage that the fire tender was kept. If there should be a fire in the day time, the horses would be removed from the shafts of the coal cart to pull the fire tender to the scene of the fire.

The first garage to be built on this site belonged to Mr Hallett and was built in 19▨.26

We come now to a row of roadside cottages, one of these was for some years a sweet shop run by Mr A. Green, and later by his son Fred.

Until a few years ago there was a brick stile between the shop and the next house, known as Tudor Close, this stile had to be crossed to reach the cottages that were to the rear of the old workhouse. Tudor Close was converted to dwellings from the coach house that belonged to the workhouse. The door at the entrance to Tudor Close is the original door to the workhouse which closed towards the end of the 19th Century. The cross-roads have altered; when I was young, a policeman always stood in the centre, on point duty to direct traffic.

This shop on the eastern corner was – after the closing of the workhouse – a butcher's, run firstly by a family named Linfield who were farmers and butchers in Ditchling for five gener-ations.

For some years it was the offices of the Ditchling Press – the presses were around the corner in South Street. The press was started as a hand press at the beginning of the 20th Century by Hilary Pepler. Later it was taken over by Westminster Press and has now moved to Burgess Hill. On our right hand side is the sweetshop and sub Post Office, the building is known as Barbers Bank, after the man of that name who ran a small bank there.

In the background can be seen the Bull Hotel. One of the five public houses in the parish, it is an interesting building and well worth a visit. Glance down the street to our left, the long house was once the home and the studio of Sir Frank Brangwyn the internationally famous artist. We cross over the road, on this corner is a building that looks Tudor, in the early 1920s a steamroller ran into it. Mr Wood the local builder was respon-sible for the repairs. It has had many uses, part of the building being used as a private residence, the other part variously used as a men's barbers, an antique shop, now as a stationers. In 1721 it is recorded that it was a pork butchers run by Nicholas Gatland and was known until recent years as Gatlands. Now it

Hilary Pepler, who launched the Ditchling Press

is called Crossways. On the other corner of the crossroads there is a grocer's, the only one left in the village that once had three.

We will stroll up the West Street, passing on our left, a bakery. This building's connection with bread goes back at least two centuries. The family that is best remembered is that of Charles Cutress, whose son became the head of Forfars. When they were here, there was a games room at the rear of the premises, where those taking tea in the tearoom or the garden could use the amenities provided.

The next shop, now an antique shop, was once a sweetshop and newsagents, run by Mr Berry of Hassocks. The fine house between it and the White Horse Inn, were a grocer's shop and its warehouse.

On the other side of the road note those two shallow arches set in the churchyard wall, these are thought to be the remains of an old blacksmith's shop.

That large sandstone set in the wall near the arches is thought to have been a pagan altar stone. I really do not know if this was so, but I do know that the village well is beneath it. The top of the well is now covered by the bricks of the path. In the 1920s a heavy lorry coming down the hill towards the crossroads broke the cover, the well was found to be about 30ft deep. At that time there was no water in it. Passing the White Horse Inn, we reach a house that looks Tudor. This house is Wing's Place. When the West Street was but a narrow track the north wing of this house came almost to the church wall. If one looks up one can see over the north door what appears to be the remains of a fireplace, and also where the floor joist must have joined. I rather think that when part of the north wing of the house was demolished, to make room for the road to be widened, part of the western wing was added. Wing's Place was for some years divided into four tenements. My family lived – for a few years – in the western end, and it was there that I was born. There was a tall chimney by our entrance door. In a summer storm of, I think, 1928, the chimney was struck by lightning, rendering it unsafe, so the stack was removed.

The outside stairway, which is on the eastern side of the house, was built towards the end of the 19th Century; a lending library was held in the upstairs room, and those wishing to borrow books used this entrance, instead of going through the house.

THE OLD HOUSE, DITCHLING, SUSSEX

Wing's Place at Ditchling. The window above the coal house is the room where the author was born

Wing's Place now belongs to the National Trust, but is only open to visitors by appointment.

The house to the west is now the vicarage. Until 1924 it was known as Sillwood House and was the home of the Botting-Tuppens who for many years farmed on the outskirts of the village.

We will cross over the road and enter the church. This is dedicated to St Margaret of Antioch. I understand from historians that there has been a place of worship on this site since the time of Alfred the Great. The church is cruciform in shape and is light and airy. It has some interesting features, a piscina, an aumbry and a sedilia; in the Abergavenny Chapel there is a monument to Henry Poole, who many years ago lived at Wing's Place. He received the house as part of his wife's dowry, he having married the daughter of Lord Abergavenny, Lord of the manor of Ditchling.

A pitch pipe is displayed in a case on the north wall of the chancel. This was used by Peter Parsons, choir master, and shoemaker of Ditchling, he also wrote the Ditchling Carol.

As we leave the church, notice in the porch a list of past vicars of the parish.

Taking the path to the north of the church, we will look at a memorial to one of the past vicars. Looking upwards we can see the initials T and H in the flintwork. They are those of Thomas Hutchinson. It was he who had this small extension built when he was vicar here in the mid 19th Century. This is his grave by the path, almost below his initials. We will take the steps down onto the green. This green now belongs to the village, thanks to a group of people who raised the money to purchase this part of Court Farm, when the farm ceased to function in 1965. The green can be hired by organisers of various functions – refreshments can be served in the barn – this helps towards the upkeep of both barn and green.

The flint outline marks the spot where there once stood a large barn. This barn was purchased by the East 15 Acting School and was transferred to Loughton in Essex where it is now known as the Harry Corbett Theatre. We leave the green, to our left stands the War Memorial to those who gave their lives in two world wars. The cost of this memorial was £119, the money being raised by public subscription. The names of those killed were carved upon the stone by Joseph Cribb in the Guild of Catholic Craftsman workshops that are on the edge of Ditchling Common.

The Reverend Norton – vicar here at the time – did not approve of the memorial being in stone; speaking in the chancel of the church, he said that he thought a memorial in the church would be more suitable. But his words were not heeded, so he refused to subscribe to the cost of the stone, instead he paid for a church room to be built in memory of those who died. It stood at the eastern end of Borers Platt. We shall pass the site later.

Beyond the memorial is the rough track known as the Drove. Before the road to Keymer was cut, that track was the only one to the villages that lay to the west of Ditchling. As the name suggest it is the one over which the drovers urged their beasts to market.

Turning to the right we find the pond. This belongs to Court House. There is always something of interest to be seen here, but not perhaps as much as in the past, when each evening – their day's work done – the farm horses were brought here to drink the water and bathe their feet, before going out into the

Mrs Bourne on her 100th birthday

field to graze.

There was always a gaggle of geese, these would waddle in strict formation, led by the gander, to take their exercise on the pond. The pond was unfenced then, but now one can lean upon the fence and watch the waterboatmen and the water fleas, dart and glide, then a duck will dive and a few water creatures will provide him with a meal. UGH! look at those water rats, hungry predators, ever scavenging for food for their ever increasing progeny, so that the eggs and the young of the many water birds are always at risk.

In the background of the pond can be seen the old village school, now thanks to the generosity of the sisters, Misses Joanna and Hilary Bourne, it now houses the Ditchling Museum. Their mother, who also lived in the village, reached the ripe old age of 102 years.

On our left is the Manor Court House, over-enlarged and swallowing up the small room in which the manor court was held. Next to it is a bungalow converted from the cart lodge. We have now reached a long house painted white. This was the farm stables, which had the pig stys on the eastern end.

The track to our right is Boddington Lane, a footpath only. We will not stroll that way, but do look over the hedge on the left of the track – that patch of scrub and weed-covered ground was once Ditchling's pride. It was the bowling green, laid out at great expense on ground that was once allotments. The Prince of Wales – later Duke of Windsor – was an honorary member. He was asked to perform the opening ceremony, he declined and sent an equerry to perform the ceremony in his place. Until that time – 1928 – the bowling club had played at a green in South Road, behind the Sundown Tea-rooms which were next to the Emanuel Chapel.

We will take the narrow lane to our left – tarmac surfaced now – but once a flint track. We skirt the bottom of Lodge Hill. I will tell you about the hill later.

The footpath on the left would take us through Bottlings – where once Ditchling cricketers played their matches – the path comes out near to the Thatched Inn, on the Keymer to Burgess Hill Road.

We stroll on between high banks on which the wild cherry trees grow, at their roots a large variety of flowers blossom. In the sandstone we can see the entrances to many burrows made by rabbits. Once many adders lived here amongst the bracken. I do not know if there are many here now.

We have reached the top of this sharp incline, so let us pause for a few moments to look over the gate on our right hand side. Not a lot to see, a few sheep grazing, but it is so peaceful. There is that lovely tile hung hovel, it gives shelter to some ponies.

Through the gap in the hedge we can see the top of Lodge Hill, on which grass and bracken grow. I was told by an old inhabitant of Ditchling that once long ago the village's wind-mill stood there. Like so many mills that stood on exposed ground, it fell to tempest blast. Let us now cross over to the stile on the left hand side of the lane. What a wonderful view; away in the distance the 200 foot spire that towers above St Hugh's Charterhouse, a monastery built by the Carthusian Monks in the mid 19th Century. Most of the windows were

The village pond, pictured in 1930

brought over from France. Its prized possession is the stole worn by St Hugh of Lincoln. The monastery lies to the south of the village of Cowfold.

Slightly nearer to us is the tower of St John's College at Hurstpierpoint. This is the middle of the three colleges built with funds raised by Nathaniel Woodward, to give a college education to the sons of tradesmen. The upper college is at Lancing, and the lower college is at Ardingly. To the south of Hurstpierpoint the hill known as Wolstonbury, the site of an ancient camp thought to be Saxon.

In line with Wolstonbury, coming this way, there stand on the summit of the South Downs two mills known the world over as Jack and Jill. Jack was restored and used by a film company. Jill is open to the public. In 1985 her sails turned again after many years of idleness and she is now once again being used to grind corn, thanks to the hard work of a band of people who raised the money for her to be restored.

I do not think anyone will have trouble in guessing the name of this field. It is the Hilly Field, it slopes so steeply. When we were young it was covered in bracken but had two clear ways,

Ditchling Bowling Green in 1928. It no longer exists

we found them grand places to toboggan. We also pronounced it Elly Field. Let us continue our stroll along the lane, passing three fine houses which were built in the 1920s. In one lived a local, hard working celebrity, William Kenning. He not only played for the local cricket and football teams, but he could also be found helping to keep the pitches in good order. He was a member of the Ditchling Choral Society of which his wife was the conductor. He also sang in the church choir. Bill, as he was known, was a keen train spotter, a hobby which he carried out sitting in this ash tree. It was while he was sitting in this tree that he died.

Near this bend in the lane, where the tarmac ends and the mud begins, once stood a fine barn in a stock yard, it unfortunately was gutted by fire. It is thought that roaming vagabonds used to sleep in the barn and maybe one of them was slightly careless with a match. The lane continues on as a muddy track towards Old Lands Mill. We go through this gate in the northern hedge, the footpath hugs the hedge on the

A steam engine passes the old barn at Lodge Hill in about 1928.
The little boy in the picture is Michael Kenning

right, but we will pause for a moment to look at that lovely old farm house, built in a style thought to be typically Sussex. It is known as Ditchling Court Gardens Farm, and it is the one that was bestowed on Ann of Cleves, among the nine that she received from Henry VIII in Sussex.

Look to the right of the house at that lovely group of conifers, every colour from the bluey greens to the golden greens, they look so much more impressive from here than they do in the garden in which they were planted in 1927. They now belong to Mr and Mrs Lewis. Mrs Lewis, is of course, better known as Dame Vera Lynn.

Let us now stroll on down the field to the stile in the eastern hedge, over the stile and into the rough farm track, a few paces will bring us to the Ditchling – Haywards Heath Road, this we cross and turning to our right we approach some wayside barns, all that are now left of the once flourishing North End Farm, these barns, having been empty for some time, have been refurbished and are in use again, not for farming, but as craft workshops called The Dumbrell-Turner Craft Centre.

We turn into the entrance on the left. This public footpath takes us through the Dumbrell Court Estate. How different it all looks now. This estate is built on the gardens and playing fields of a school. This school was started in 1882 by Mrs Dumbrell after her husband John was thrown from his horse and killed while riding on the South Downs. The school gained a worldwide reputation for its high standard. Many parents doing terms of office overseas, left their daughters in Mrs Dumbrell's care.

In its last years it became a preparatory school. The school finally closed its doors in 1982.

In 1935 a fire destroyed some of the farm buildings. Mr Joseph Holman – known as Jack – at great risk to himself, entered the blazing building and led the bull to safety. Anyone knowing anything about animals will know the extent of this brave act, for the bull, being chained in the heart of the fire, was maddened with fear. Jack was assisted in this remarkable rescue by Geoffrey Williams, who although physically disabled, helped by trying to put out the fire. For these brave acts both men received awards, Jack receiving a silver medal and diploma of merit from the Royal Society for the Prevention of Cruelty to Animals, and Geoffrey receiving a Diploma of Merit.

We now stroll onwards passing the eastern hedge of the Blue House, once the home of Amy Sawyer, the playwright and artist. This brings us to East Gardens. When I was young, this track was known as Blind Lane, in those days it came to a dead end, now one can walk through to East End Lane. We will take the right hand fork. Behind this brick wall was once the yard of Woods, the builders of many of Ditchling's fine houses. I am told that one of the sheds was for a time used as a mission room.

We have now reached the corner of this rough track, on our left is the meeting house of the Society of Friends, not so long ago it was the slaughterhouse of Slater the butchers.

This next house is Candles, takng its name from the fact that candles were once made here. On our right, now part of a private residence but for many years a saddlers and shoe and boot makers, the last person to ply that trade here was Mr A. Tomsett.

On the other side of the road, the eastern entrance to Boddington Lane. Where the Colt bungalow stands, once stood the church room, that I mentioned earlier, it did have a plaque

J. Holman and G. Williams receive their bravery awards
from the Rev C. P. Williams

over the door stating that it had been built as a memorial, I do
not know what happened to the plaque when the room was
demolished.

We turn to our left passing an antique shop, which was for
many years a butchers shop, Slaters, Jefferies and lastly
Andrews. It was from the balcony over the south window that
for many years the proclamation was read to open Ditchling's
village fair.

We can see the length of the High Street; how busy it is, but
when I was young there was so little traffic that boys could spin
their tops up and down the street for long periods without
having to give way to anything except an inquisitive dog.

Notice those pollarded lime trees. It is from them that the
house behind gets its name. For some years Mr and Mrs A. E.
Sinden, the parents of three famous children lived. Joy, a mime
artist, Leon a straight actor, and Donald, an actor and film star.
Rosemary Pepler, the daughter of Esther Meynell the well
known author, lives in the house now.

The house next to it was once like its neighbours, but someone in recent years has put a false front on it, trying to make it look Tudor. It is thought to be the house in which a notorious smuggler named Conds lived, and it is now known as Conds Cottage.

The next house down has a plaque on it to say Eric Gill the sculptor lived there for a short time.

We will turn into the road on our left, East End Lane. On the right, now a private house, was the sub post office, this was run for many years by James Vincent. When he retired the shop and post office were taken over by Fred and Phyllis Edwards, Fred had worked for Mr Vincent since he left school, in all Fred was in that office for more than 50 years. This large red brick building next to the old post office is now known as Dymocks Manor, and is home to several families, but for many years it was Ditchling's vicarage. It was enlarged from a small house, standing well back from the road and surrounded by lovely gardens. The extensions were carried out by the Reverend Norton, this red brick extension near to the footpath was his children's nursery. On the other side of the road, Dove Cottage, once a Beulah Chapel, built by George Grenyer in 1867, now a private house. There was at one time under the floor, the bath in which people were immersed at their baptism. We have now reached the Scout Headquarters. This was converted from three cottages known as Ditchling Gardens. It was here that the Edwards family lived for about 125 years.

On our right a row of cottages built in 1814, as a free school for boys by Mr Chatfield, the building was enlarged later so that girls could also attend.

We enter the Twitten. On our left some very old cottages, named Forge Cottages, for some years a forge stood near here. On our right, the Unitarian Meeting House, in its first years this was a strict Baptist Chapel. It was erected about 1672 by the same Chatfield family that built the schools. The building has been enlarged many times. The bath for the Baptisms is now sealed under the floor.

This part of the burial ground was once the playing ground for the school. On our left a small burial plot, all members of the Browne family. All spelt with the end E except one, the reason for this is the stonemason did not allow himself room, so he carved the missing E on the other side of the stone. They were all members of a family of mercers who traded in

East End Lane at Ditchling

Ditchling and at Lewes. For many years there was always a Browne on the board of Trustees of the Meeting House.

Until 1822 there was no footpath along the part of the Twitten that we have just trod, it came from the south and ended here. In that year James Browne purchased from Stephen Andrews a strip of land, because the new owners of the land to the south of the chapel closed a path that came from the side of the Bull Hotel, saying that there was no right of way there, so this left the Meeting house with no entrance. Notice that the coping stones on the wall on the right are turned – this was once the stile to the path that was closed.

We pass Rookery Cottages on our left, and come to the south end of the Twitten. This large house stands on what was once the gardens to Rookery Cottages that we have just passed. Many dwellings about here have the word Rookery in their names, so I think that before they were built there must have been a large group of trees about here where the rooks built their homes. Did you know that a colony of rooks nest are called a building! sounds very suitable doesn't it.

This road is the B2116 which we will be crossing and re-crossing several times during our stroll.

Ditchling Common in the 1920s.

Stroll to the top of the South Downs

THERE before us is Ditchling Village Hall. We will not cross over to it, we turn to the left and cross to Lexden House. This was once a pebble-dash house surrounded by laurels. At that time it was school for young ladies run by the Misses Anne and Elizabeth Capon. The house was enlarged in the mid 1930s.

For a long time Lexden was the last house to the east of the village, from here onwards the road was just a narrow track, widened about 1927/8. The fields at that time belonged to Gunn's Farm.

We will enter this tarmac surfaced lane, which is just to the east of Lexden. When I was young the lane was far more attractive, being a grass track with a field gate at each end, each gate had a squeeze stile at its side. When the plot of land on the east of the lane was sold as a building plot, the residents on the other side of the road took the purchasers to court to try to get the building stopped, for they said a house there would spoil their view. They did not win and the house was built. Funny to think about it, their house had only been built a few years before. Up until the house – Nuthurst was built, the field had been known as Fairfield, for it was the site on which the roundabouts and swings and other sideshows that were a part of every village fair, were placed. Later the fairs, in conjunction with the produce show, were held in the Star Field, which is the North Road next to the North Star beer house.

We have now reached the south end of the lane, the cottage on the right was built about 1935/6. The house on the left is Little Ash. It was Converted from the coach house belonging to Ashburnham, a house in the Lewes Road.

We now enter the fields of Gospels Farm. This farm was once of a far greater size. Now it is of five fields known respectively as St Matthew, St Mark, St Luke, St John and the Epistles. The small farm house – the entrance to which was in the South Road – was knocked down to make way for two larger houses to be built.

Sally Porter

Oxeye Daisies

The stalwarts of the Ditchling Cricket Club in the Twenties

These fields, named after the four Apostles, make up a large square, divided by neat hedgerows into four smaller squares. These fields are now given over to grazing for horses.

How different to the time when I was young and the farm was run by Mr L. Stenning and his wife; they were full of life, with ducks on the pond and a dairy herd.

In St John's, during the dormant months, the village team played their football matches, but they had to vacate the field in early April to the cows who grazed then sat and ruminated there between milking times. There were no changing rooms for the players, they came in their playing kit and went home in all their dirt. I wonder what visiting teams thought! Throughout the summer months, St Matthew not only provided grazing for the cattle, it also provided a pitch for the local cricket team. The players had to round up the cows and confine them to the milking parlour, and then with shovels clean up the field before they could play. Many a match was enlivened by a player slipping on a badly cleaned patch. The field called St Mark is the meadow to our left, this was – as far as I can remember – always grazed early in the year and then left to be

Sally Po[r]

Ragged Robin

Sally Porter

Buttercup

Sally Porter

Wild Rose

Sally Porter

Hedge Mustard

Sally Porter

Red Clover

Ground Ivy

Sally Porter

hayed for winter feeding.

Having walked diagonally across St Matthew, we cross the stile in the south east corner and we enter St Luke. The meadow of herbs. It is in this field that herbs grow in multi coloured profusion. I often wonder, did those monks who so long ago cleared the scrubland to make these meadows, choose this quarter to sow those bountiful seeds and then name it for the holy physician St Luke. I wonder also does his spirit come each year and bless this herbal patch? At all times of the year some healing plants can be found growing here.

Although in the morning sun this meadow looks inviting, it is in the evening that it can be found in all its glory, and at that time the perfume – a mixture of sweet and pungent smells – is a tantalising puzzle. How many different kinds of herbs can we find? The pink flowers of the ragged robin jostling with the white flowered Oxeyed Daisy and the smaller field daisies, also the rye grass. Nestling at their roots are the blue flowers of the ground ivy, intermingled with the red or white flowers of the clover – this is not a native of our country but an import from Holland.

The rust red of the sorrel and the golds of the buttercups and of the dandelions. Here also the yellow rattle, in the evening time – when the sun has ripened them – as the seeds leave the pods, they do indeed rattle.

Near to the hedgerows grow the wild carrot and the cow parsley with its lovely white lacey flower heads. Some people call it ladies lace. In other districts it is known as Queen Anne's Lace.

When we were children we found the stems, when dry, made lovely peashooters. There also grow the stinging nettles, with the handy docks close by. Also the comfrey and the hedge mustard, all of which had their uses. The trees in the hedgerows themselves must also have been planted for the various uses to which they could be put, also I think for the superstitions connected with them.

The hazels, showing now their diminutive red flowers, which later in the year bear succulent nuts.

The honeysuckle, the flowers of which add such a delicate perfume to a bowl of pot-pourri. If one of the suckers is wound tightly around a straight stem of a neighbouring hazel and thus allowed to grow for six to seven years and then cut, the result is

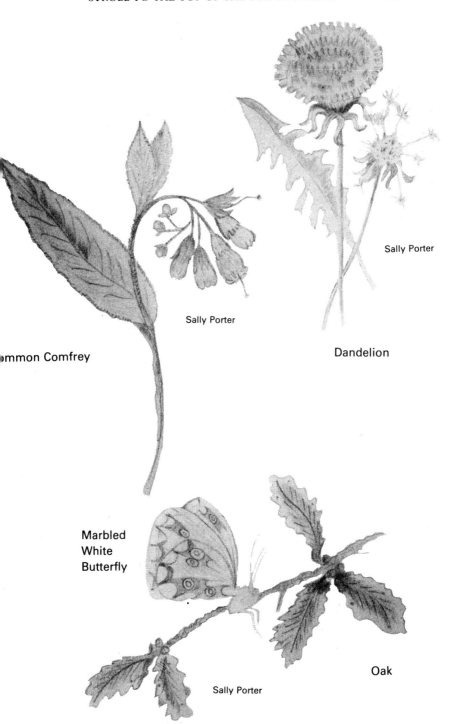

Sally Porter

Dandelion

Sally Porter

mmon Comfrey

Marbled
White
Butterfly

Oak

Sally Porter

a nicely turned walking stick.

The crab apples, whose fruit is small and green and so very sour, but what a lovely jelly they make.

The hawthorn's pink and white flowers herald the red berries called haws, but known locally as eggasses, these make a really potent drink. The delicate pale pink petals of the wild rose – called by some dog rose. The fruit known as hips, make a vitamin filled syrup, good for growing children.

In days of yore the suckers of the wild rose were used in the making of beehives, and the roots were used to make Briar tobacco pipes. The blackthorn, whose fruit are known as sloes, make a drink fit for any king. Some people add gin to the syrup, but in my opinion this spoils the flavour.

Just look at the profusion of creamy white flowers on the elders. The flowers of these sweeten many other fruits if added to them whilst they are cooking. They also make a refreshing drink, but some blossoms should be left to berry, for the syrup made from them eases the pain of winter coughs. Remember before picking flowers or berries, to bow to the tree and ask the elder witch for permission to do so, or she will be very angry. The wood from the elder tree should never be taken into a house to be burnt lest evil odours fill the house.

The holly berries, in the hardness of winter time, feed our native birds; the leaves distilled were at one time used to ease the pain of dropsy. Its branches – with weights attached – would before the time of chimney sweeps, be dropped down chimney stacks to clear the clinging soot; this soot would be used in gardens as a deterrent to slugs. No wonder the ancients thought that the holly tree was one of good omen, for beside these uses they also thought that they would keep rats away from their grain.

As you can see, the hedge also contains a number of ash trees, for it was thought that they would guard a field from snakes; and the bark distilled would cure all manner of ills.

That buzz that we can hear is the song of the bees, who are busy collecting pollen from the herbs; for all their hard work, they are rewarded by humans taking the resulting honey.

The path that we are treading crosses diagonally through this meadow of herbs; I wonder how many generations of little girls have set upon this path making daisy chains, and how many little boys, chasing after butterflies, have paused at hearing the sound of grasshoppers, have stopped to watch them jump from one stem to another, and have then seen the tiny ants busy dragging some object twice their own size back to their own anthill home.

I wonder yet again how many of those boys when grown into their teens, have stolen a kiss from the girl of their choice, whilst holding a buttercup under her chin, in the pretence of seeing if she liked butter. And she tried to find out the type of man that she would marry with the help of the flowers of the rye grass.

We have now reached the stile in the south east corner, at its side a few roots of quaking grass – some times called todling grass. The tiny purplish brown seed pods looking like fairy shoes. The slightest breeze shakes them and it looks as if a fairy is really dancing in them. We climb the stile and enter the eastern end of the Epistles. Let us leave the path for a moment and look in that small drainage pond. It is almost overgrown with weeds now, for it is thought the water in such ponds is harmful to cattle, so the ponds are no longer kept clean. When I was young the pond was clear, and that alder was in its prime; its branches cast dark shadows over the water, as if to shelter the creatures that lived in the pond water. I remember jam jars held by little hands being quickly filled with water as the children tried to catch the wriggling inhabitants, to take to school for nature study. On the reeds there, a pair of mallard have built their untidy nest, a miscellaneous gathering of sticks and dried grass. Almost invisible sits the dowdy duck, blending in to her surroundings. Let us leave her in peace and return to the path.

Nye Lane, is that track to the left that we can see over the hedge. Difficult now to visualise the waggons using it as they did in the past, although in recent times the Manpower

The Robin

Services Commission has set lads to work laying hardcore upon tough plastic sheeting in an effort to keep the mud down. There has been a great increase in the number of horse riders using the lane in the last few years. Although we do not have the fox hunters around here now.

Most of the time the lane runs with water, as if it were a brook. Its banks are lined with moss; violets, white, blue and pink, peep out from their deep green leaves. Ferns are interspersed with clumps of pale yellow primroses which also nestle in the soft green moss. On the top of the bank in the hedgerow, the dogwood with its crimson branches contrasts with the dark green of the spiky blackthorn.

For many years the village refuse – collected by a local farmer – was tipped in the field to the east of the lane, this was after the brickworks ceased to function. Apparently the clay was not suitable for brick making, so the project was short-lived.

Look at that cheeky robin! He has built his nest in that old kettle; it must have slipped down from the old tip, or maybe bottle collectors have been scavenging nearby. Can you see in the bank, just above the kettle, a dome shaped nest? It belongs to the little wren. Did you know that the male wren always builds two nests, so his little wife may choose in which she would like to live and bring up their young. They are reputed to be the king and queen of birds.

We are now skirting Nye Wood. It is from this small triangular shaped wood that – under the terms of an old bequest – the working people of Ditchling may cut pea and bean sticks, but only as many as may be carried, no carts may be used.

The track forks here. We take the one to the right. The one to the left is the bridleway known as Wellcroft Lane. The bluebells down that way give the finest display of any place I know. Unfortunately for walkers, the path is for the most part of the year impassable. So we walk to the right, skirting the eastern edge of Jointure Wood, that delightful scent that seems to fill the air is from the wild hyacinth, its mauvy-blue flowers interspersed with the pinky-white flowers of the wood anemones, making a beautiful carpet for the trees that tower above them.

On our left is a chicken farm, and next to it a red brick house called High Croft, once the home of the sisters of General Earl Haigh, the man who founded the British Legion (now called The Royal British Legion). A few yards further on a much

David and Anne Mills
in their vineyard.

newer house, Claycroft, and the famous Ditchling vineyard –
the wines from these vines have won many awards. It was the
advent of this undertaking that resulted in the bridlepath that
we are treading being made up with hardcore, so that it is not
the quagmire that it had been since the waggons stopped using
it.

On the right hand side, a disused marl pit. In winter time and
early spring, the pit is full of water, here mallard build their
untidy nest and the eggs laid by the dowdy duck hatch, the
resulting young learn to swim and to forage for food. In the late
spring they fly away to find some other watery spot. I have seen
as many as six pairs of mallard swimming here with their
young.

It really looks like a man made lake that has been landscaped,
with the wealth of flowers and trees around its banks.

In the early 1930s there was a fire at Coombe Wood House –
which stood on the south bank of the pit. Ditchling's Fire
Brigade arrived in good time, but the house was gutted,

Harebell

S. M. Hall

S. M. Hall

Cowslip

because the pit was dry and there was no water to be had. This was before water hydrants, or the use of foam. How lucky we are with so many new inventions.

We have now reached the T junction of Nye Lane and Underhill Lane. This lane runs from Offham to Clayton.

On the Downs above us can be clearly seen the silhouette of Gladstone's Head, carved at a time when he was Britain's Prime Minister. The grass has grown again now and I feel that it looks better now than when the chalk predominated, although if the surrounding shrubbery is not soon cut, no one will recognise it.

We turn to the left and after a few yards turn into a lane on the right. This lane leads us to the slype. What is a slype? Well, it is a path on which one can walk without being seen by any person standing above or in the valley below, unfortunately, this one has become very overgrown. Walkers like to walk on the bank above, where they can see the fine view of the Weald.

On our right is a nature reserve, where can be seen some of the chalk hill flowers and some of our loveliest butterflies. Let us climb on to the bank on the left, and look into the valley.

What can we see? On the roof of that thatched cottage, two ducks, looking as if they are about to fly away, but they will not do so, they are made of wire and straw. When a thatcher finishes a roof, be it cottage or barn, he weaves his trade mark. The thatcher that remade that roof uses mallard as his. I wonder how many people have thought them real, and have watched to see them fly away?

On these slopes, for many decades, the sweet smelling cowslips, made each spring a carpet of golden yellow. The local people's love of cowslip wine – made from the tiny petals – almost wiped out the plants, but now, in this more enlightened age, the plants are growing again and are increasing in numbers.

Later in the year the grass will be hazed with blue as harebells, scabious and the rampions blossom.

There are few sheep here now, but in the last century the hills were alive with the sound of "Baa-ing", for it is recorded that 1,500 sheep grazed here. These sheep belonged to Mr Botting a flock master who lived at Westmeston Place Farm. He had one of the largest flocks of South Down sheep in the county.

Some people have written of the lovely life of the shepherds, forgetting, perhaps, that these men wandered the Downs in rain, snow and howling gales, besides the balmy spring days or the days of blazing hot sun, contending not only with all manner of ailments that sheep are prey to, but also they had to keep their charges free from packs of dogs and the marauding fox.

Onward now for the last few yards of the upward climb, here the slype meets the upper Beacon Road, we follow this for a few yards until we reach the summit.

Westmeston's only car park is on our right, this was laid out at the expense of members of the National Trust, who were given the piece of land by Mrs Rhodes-Moorehouse in memory of her father Sir Stephen Demetriadi who once owned many acres of this lovely downland.

We will go over the stile which is on our left with a bridlegate beside it. These stiles and gates have been erected by voluntary labour, the materials having been provided by the Countryside Commission. Looking to the south we can see the sea at Brighton, slightly to the south east is the flag pole at Brighton racecourse.

Still further to the south east, there stand Have Brow, Short Brow, Rough Brow, Bran Point, Flagstaff Point, Bailly Hill and West Hill Brow, the hills that make up the range known as the Seven Sisters.

Just look at that skylark! Soaring so high, trilling in flight and then breaking into song as it hovers above us. We must be careful where we put our feet, for the skylark does not build a safe nest as do most other birds, they just pull together dried grasses on the ground, and there lay their eggs, prey to the carelessly placed feet of cattle and of humans.

That indentation of mud was once the dewpond, but with piped water for the cattle, the dewponds have fallen into disrepair. It was on this slope that for a short period in the early 1930s that a few gliding enthusiasts tried out their skills – with little success. They soon moved over to Firle Beacon.

On such a lovely day as this, it is difficult to imagine the wind howling up here as it does at times. I think it is this wind and the suddenly falling mist that have given rise to the legend of the Witches Hounds that some folk say roam this part of the Downs. No, I have never heard or seen them, but I have been

Mr Godley, shepherd of the Dumbrell estate's flock, in 1914

View of the Weald from the Downs above Westmeston

caught in the suddenly falling mist and heard the wind howling. It certainly gives one a weird feeling.

What I have seen, is the ghost of a Saxon Chieftain walking along this ridge. The first time that I saw him, I thought maybe a film company was making a film here, only there did not seem to be many people about. As I watched him, he seemed to fade, leaving me puzzled. The second time that I saw him, was after a lapse of some years, he was standing on this brow looking out across the Weald. Admiring the view! Or watching for the enemy?

I later made some enquiries and I found that the Brighton and Hove Archaeology Society had – in the mid 1920s – opened up a single grave not far from here, this contained the skeleton of what they thought from the things buried with him in the grave probably that of a Saxon Chieftain. Did the opening of the grave release the spirit and allow him to once again guard over his tribe? Interesting to note that there was a Saxon settlement at Pidelingworth just south of here. This belonged to the Countess Gutha – herself a Dane – she was married to Earl Goodwin. They were the parents of King Harold II so it was possible that he came from that camp.

Let us now walk over to the stile that is in the fence above the northern escarpment of the Downs. This stile is wide enough to sit upon or just to lean against. As this is my favourite viewing place, take your ease and let me describe the scene to you.

The Viewing Place

THERE laid out before us, a pleasing patchwork of colours and shapes, not the modern type of patchwork, that which is all neatly cut and sewn, but that as worked by generations of country women. The pieces of all shapes and sizes, not a piece of cloth was cut, so not an inch of cloth was lost. Then every piece was neatly sewn together with feather stitching. So the Weald looks to me, each patch of earth neatly outlined with hedgerows.

The various shades of browns denote the different types of soil turned up by the plough. These patches of brown turn to patches of green as the various crops start to grow and they will later turn to yellow and to gold as the crops ripen.

To me it is the patterned pieces that hold the interest, of these I will pick out those that I think are of the greatest interest. Starting in the far distance, dimly seen, the highest ridges of the North Downs. The dark oblong patch in front of the Downs is Ashdown Forest, one that is almost denuded of trees, for many centuries ago the trees were felled and alas none were replanted to replace them. Their limbs were used – according to the type of tree – for charcoal, or to feed the bloomeries and the furnaces of the iron industry. The mighty trunks, on wains, were drawn by oxen, along the trackway through the forest and the Weald and so up the Borstals of the South Downs, and then onwards to the shipyards, to be used in the building of England's mighty fleet.

Looking forward slightly to the south east of that dark patch to a small green patch with a white windmill upon it. That is the smock mill at Chailey, said to stand in the middle of Sussex. It stands to the south-east side of Chailey Heritage; this was once part of a workhouse, now, greatly enlarged, it is a craft school for children with some physical disability.

This school was started in 1903 by Mrs Kimmin and has come a long way from its small beginnings with just seven boys. Now thousands of children – boys and girls – have

Skating on the pond at Ditchling Common

received treatment and training there. The Heritage chapel can not be seen from here, but it is interesting as one of the oak doors was made by one of those first seven boys. There is a road of remembrance and a memorial in the grounds to the 28 boys of the Heritage who gave their lives in the 1914–18 war. A wonderfully descriptive poem has been written about the work done there. It is called the Master Shipwright and tells of those first nurses and doctors' prayers for guidance, and how those prayers were answered. I do not know if copies can be obtained now.

On the patch in front of the mill can be seen a church with a tall spire that is the church of St Peter's, Chailey. It sits on the edge of the common and was restored in 1878/9. The weather-vane bears the date 1772. Now looking to the left of the mill, a patch with a tall chimney upon it, set amongst a cluster of buildings, that is St Francis Hospital. This hospital stands slightly to the south east of Haywards Heath and was built as an extension to the Brighton Hospital for the treatment of the mentally sick; Hurstwood Park Hospital stands in the same patch and soon there will be more rooftops there, for the new

Mid Sussex Hospital is being built on the site.

To the south-west of that tall chimney, we can see a very much patterned piece, showing many rooftops. That is a fairly new town known as Burgess Hill. This town was made from parts of the villages of Clayton, Keymer and St Johns Common, the last name seems to have been completely obscured. Burgess Hill has now become the main shopping place for this part of Sussex, holding a market on two days of the week. To the west of the town there is a small industrial estate for light industry.

In line with those rooftops, coming back to the right, an expansive patch of green, that is Ditchling Common. In spring time a blueish haze predominates the green, a carpet of wild hyacinths in bloom.

The bracken was at one time cut for animal bedding, but it is not used now except by those growing azaleas.

This common was at one time famous for its chalybeate spring, the waters of which were thought to cure rheumatism.

In the north-west corner of the common is a gibbet, known as Jacob's Post. It was there that the corpse of a pedlar – by name Jacob Harris – was hung in chains, after he had been found guilty of the murders of three persons at a nearby inn known as The Royal Oak. His trial took place at the assizes at Horsham in West Sussex, where having been found guilty of "murders most foul" he was hanged. The body was brought back to the common to hang in chains, as was the custom in those days; this was supposed to be a warning to other would-be wrongdoers.

The old people would say that a piece of the wood from the gibbet carried in the pocket would guard the carrier from tooth-ache. They cut so many slivers from it to sell to gullible people that the gibbet collapsed, it has been renewed in recent times. On the south-eastern side of the common, a very large house, once known as Purchase Manor House, now known as St George's Retreat, the old house is now St Mary's. The estate was purchased in 1868 by the sisters of the order of St Augustine. After much rebuilding – including a chapel – they opened as a retreat for persons with some type of mental problem. They now have a section for elderly persons, who can go there to convalesce, or stay as long term residents.

On the southern side of the common, there is now a car park

S. M. Hall

Hard Headed Knapweed

and nature trail. This is a pleasant place to stroll, there is a pond – in which in days gone by boys learnt to swim, and skate if the ice allowed. The pond has been cleared of weed and rubbish and stocked with fish for the local angling club members, a number of water fowl can be seen on the pond.

On the eastern edge of the common, there is a small industrial estate built on the site of the old brick and tile terracotta workings. This yard was famous for making terracotta Wyverns.

Slightly to the south of this but still on the common, are six semi-detached cottages, these are known as The City. I do not know why they were given this name. It is most likely a Sussex joke. On the south west of the common, there is a small group of community workshops, these were started in 1912 by Eric Gill, Desmond Chute and Hilary Pepler and they are still being used today by craftsmen, all of them of the Roman Catholic faith.

One landmark that can no longer be seen is the Calvary which stood 20 feet high on top of the Spoil Bank near to the railway line. This was carved by Eric Gill and placed there in 1919. It stood on that grassy knoll until 1950. Unfortunately vandals were carving graffiti on it, so the members of the Guild decided to take it down. As there was no other site on which to place it, after much thought, it was sold to the Rensselar Newham Politec in Troy, New York State, America, where the figure, having been removed from the cross, hangs over the high altar.

From the common let your eyes travel south. A large patterned piece with a church with a spire, that is the village of Ditchling – that we left this morning – the area around the village is thought to have been the hunting ground of Kings.

To the north of the church, the small green hill, called Lodge Hill, I said when we passed it that I would tell you of it. It is said by learned men to be the site of an ancient burial ground of the people of Dicel, from whom the village is said to get its name. Since 1951 it has been the setting for the Ditchling Pageant which is enacted on the base of the hill every tenth year. There is a wide flat strip at the base of the hill, thought to have been part of a Roman road.

This hill is remembered by those so fortunate to have spent their childhood in the village, as the best place to toboggan.

Slightly to the north-west of the hill, there is a large green patch with a white windmill upon it. That is Old Land Mill. This mill stands on the boundary of Ditchling and Keymer; the mill has been renovated many times since it ceased to be a working mill. On one occasion the repair bill was paid by Mr Ferguson – the builder responsible for the Hassocks Homes Estate – and for this gesture he was given permission to use a picture of the mill on his business stationery. The mill is once again in disrepair and funds are being sought for the work to be done. It seems to me to be a very expensive antique. The last miller to work the mill was Mr D. Driver.

Now let us look to the right of Ditchling. There are many plain coloured pieces, then there are a few with scattered buildings on them, that is Hayleigh Farm, once the home of the keeper of the royal park. This park is mentioned in the Domesday Book. It was in the year 1931 that a very virulent outbreak of foot and mouth disease, which spreads through a herd of cattle so quickly, and causes so much suffering that all cattle have to be destroyed. Mr Springate, whose family had farmed at Hayleigh for many years, gave up farming. The present house dates from the 16th Century. The farm is presently famous for its pigs and its strawberries.

Now look slightly to the right of the farm, another patch with a church upon it. That is the parish church of Streat. Its dedication name is unknown, although one source gives it as All Saints.

It has some interesting memorials, some to the Dobell family who owned a large part of Sussex for many generations. Their history can be found in the Sussex Records Office at Lewes.

The lychgate is a memorial, built by the Fitzhugh family who towards the end of the 19th Century lived at Streat Place. Under a yew tree in the churchyard there is a very long grave, that of a giant; or a mother with a child buried at her feet.

Looking from our viewing place, as if it is joined to the church, we see the house known as Streat Place. This house had its beginning in Tudor times, but is mainly Jacobean with a Victorian extension. Like most old houses it is said to have many ghosts, for an account of these I asked Elsie and Winifred Sawyer, who, when in their teens were maids in the house. The following is the account they gave me:

"One day as we were taking the afternoon tea into the draw-

ing room, Mrs Swift, the mistress of the house, who was standing by the window, looking out into the garden, said: 'Elsie,
who is that woman? What is she doing in our garden?' We both
looked out of the window and saw a woman who seemed to be
wearing a whimple type headdress; her gown was long and
black; at the mistress' bidding we ran out into the garden but
could see no trace of the woman. We asked the gardener, who
was working there, he said he had seen no-one. The woman
had vanished, if she had been human it would not have been
possible for her to have entered or left the garden without
having been seen.

"On another occasion – whilst the family were away – we
maids made sure that the house was secure for the night. As we
sat talking in the kitchen, the room suddenly filled with the
smell of cigar smoke. Knowing that we had searched and then
locked the door of each room, we were puzzled. We lit a lantern
– no electric light then – and searched the surrounding grounds,
but could find no-one, what really surprised us was the fact that
we could not smell the smoke in any place but the kitchen."

There are also reported to be three other ghosts about the
house which I have heard about from other sources.

One is the figure of a man dressed in the garb of a Cavalier,
he rushes into the entrance hall and vanishes up the large fireplace. Other reports are that he enters the hall riding a horse, he
also vanishes up the same chimney. Horse as well!

There has also been seen a lady dressed in grey, she carries a
parasol, she suddenly appears, walking to the centre of the front
lawn, then she vanishes.

On winter's evenings there can be heard at times, the sound
of a heavy carriage pulled by horses. It seems to stop at what
was once the front door, then after a few minutes can be heard
moving away.

This driveway has not been the entrance to the house for
about 200 years, and is so overgrown that no carriage in
modern times could traverse it.

I think Streat Place has a surfeit of ghosts don't you? So let us
move on to look at another patch. The one in front of the
church has a white monument upon it, a memorial to those
men of Westmeston and Streat who gave their lives in the wars.
Still looking to the right, a large patch of green, this changes its
pattern often, sometimes horses can be seen racing upon it, at

other times it is patterned with tents and caravans, when folk from many nations come for the Downs Bible Gathering. The patch is of course Plumpton racecourse.

Coming forward a little, almost to the foot of the Downs, an oblong patch with a variety of shaped buildings upon it, that is Plumpton Agriculture College, with the tiny church of St Michael almost hidden in its midst. This church – the parish church of Plumpton – is well worth a visit. On its walls are paintings similar to those at Clayton and Hardham churches.

Coming back this way to the left, again sparsely patterned pieces, others with a few cattle or sheep on them, then there is a patch with a number of rooftops showing above the trees. Those are of Middleton Court and New Middleton House – mostly referred to as Middleton Manor. Middleton Court, is a block of flats built in the 1970s for young people with some type of mental problems. We will be passing both on our way home and I will tell you about them then.

The green patch in front of those houses is often patterned with figures dressed in white, for it is on that patch that

The Street, Westmeston, in 1909

The church of St Martin of Tours at Westmeston

Westmeston and Streat cricketers play their at home matches. Almost below this viewing place, another patch with a church upon it – the parish church of Westmeston, dedicated to St Martin of Tours. We can see the small bell tower with its Sussex Cap quite clearly, the date on the weathervane is 1773. I am so pleased that the Victorians did not add a spire, as they did to so many small churches. We will take a closer look at it when we descend the hill.

Behind the church, we can just see a fine house known as the Old Rectory, not as aged as the name suggests, for it was built after a fire destroyed part of the old house in 1845. It is so called because since 1908 the rectory has been at Streat, at that time the two parishes were combined under one rector.

Now look to the north west of the church, a patch with a red roof upon it, that is the roof of Westmeston Place. Another house thought to have had its beginnings in Tudor times. Like most old houses it has been enlarged many times, the house is thought to have been a hospice, run firstly by the brotherhood of St Michael, whose college was at South Malling in Lewes. It was then taken over by the monks of St Pancras, also of Lewes.

The house is thought to have once belonged to the Michelbourne family, who once owned a large part of Sussex.

The small blue patch to the west of the house is a pond, also thought to have been made by those monks, as their stew pond. It was here that many of the local lads learnt to swim. In years gone by many sheep were dipped in the pond.

Still looking to the west, those neat rows of brown – soon to turn green – are the vineyard that we passed on the way up here. It is a fairly new venture this growing of grapes for wine here in Sussex. But is it so new? The Romans were here, as we know from the traces of the roads they made that have been found hereabouts. They introduced the vine into this country, so I feel sure they had vineyards here.

It is not just the seasons that change the colour of these patterns. The sky also has a great effect upon them, for according to the density of the clouds, the colours are sometimes light and sometimes dark.

I think that it is the variation of colours, and that on every visit some changes have taken place, that make this my favourite viewing place. I wonder what the Saxon Chieftain thinks of the changes that have taken place from the time when he stood guard here, and all he could see would be forest land.

Let us sit here and eat our lunch, and enjoy the view, you may see some patches that I have not described to you.

Look at the kestrel, almost stationary, as it hovers above us, it might almost be suspended on a wire, until it spots its prey, a mouse, small birds or even spiders. It then dives with incredible speed giving its prey no time to creep away.

There goes the cuckoo, they always sing whilst flying. I have noticed that besides being too lazy to build their own nest for their offspring they never seem to get up in time to join the first of the dawn chorus.

Into Westmeston

REFRESHED? Then let us descend the hill, but not too quickly or we shall miss the large variety of flowers that grow here. Some, like the yellow-flowered ragwort, and the mauve flowers of the hard headed knapweed, grow so tall and straight, it would be difficult to miss them. Others so small, but each so perfect, need to be looked for. No matter in which season one comes this way, there are always some blossoms to be seen, the very small ones like the squincy wort and the bedstraw. Do you know how the bedstraw came by its name? No! It was because in olden times people travelled by foot or if fortunate by donkey, there were few inns, even for those who could afford them. So it was that each traveller carried with them a palliasse – no not a friendly donkey – but a hessian bag. This was about two foot wide and four foot long. The poor travellers filled theirs with dried grasses or, if they could find it, straw. Ladies had theirs filled with the prolific sweet smelling herbs, because of this usage the plant became known as Ladies Bedstraw. A lovely country story isn't it?

Those yellow flowers are called sow thistles; apparently when pigs roamed wild, and had to search for their own food, they loved them and the plants almost died out. Then there is the thyme, an insignificant little flower, but if one should step on a clump of their leaves, what a wonderful scent arises!

Look at those shrubs on the escarpment, the creamy white flowers of the guelder rose. In autumn time the berries turn to red and to black on the same head.

The pale pink blossoms of the wild rose, the deep cream flowers of the elder, the pink and white flowers of the hawthorn, all not only a picture now. In autumn time they are all covered in berries, making a wonderful store of food for the wild birds.

When I was a young girl, I walked these slopes with our Sunday School teacher – Miss Grace Brown – and in one walk we found and she identified 120 different types of grasses.

Members of the Westmeston choir, who were awarded
a certificate of merit at the Lewes Music Festival in 1952

We are now standing above the Westmeston chalk pit. Just look at all those rabbits scampering down at the base; can you see any black ones? There is at least one black furred rabbit in each colony. I asked my father why this should be. He told me: "The black one be the parson, no real country man would kill one." Again I asked why. He replied: "Because the flesh be tough and laid long on the chest and kept repeating like some parsons' sermons." My father was a great man for a joke so I still do not know the real reason.

The chalk pit itself is very overgrown with grass and shrubs. Chalk is not often quarried nowadays. At one time it was quarried not only for lime burning, but also for drainage. Before the coming of the combine harvester – when farmers ricked their crops to be threshed at a later date – the chalk was used as a base for the ricks.

This path connects with Westmeston's borstall, a strange name for these curving tracks of the South Downs. Many explanations for the name have been given, and I am no wiser than others, but I do admit that I do not know. I think that they were made by the oxen that drew the timbers from the Weald to the shipyards, for an oxen would have walked curvingly upwards, they would never have pulled their loads straight upwards, they swayed along, and so the tracks wound upwards like giant meat hooks. The only animal that runs straight upwards – in this part of the world – is the hare.

In that cluster of trees and brambles, on our left, are the remains of some lime kilns, they had – when in use – iron chimneys coming out of the side of the hill; they came down early this century, when lime burning on a small scale was found to be uneconomic; these small hillocks were made from the residue of the lime burning activities. We take the downward arm of the borstall, it wanders between high banks where at all times of the year some things of interest can be found.

In spring time, wild hyacinths and the sweet smelling violets, the red flowers of the campion, known as bachelor buttons, also the wild parsley interspersed with ferns.

There are the wild cherry trees above them, at the moment a cloud of white blossoms. One can not eat the fruit for they are hard and sour. The wood has always been in great demand, for the grain when polished is lovely. Articles made from the wood were very expensive, for the trees do not grow to a very large size, tobacco pipes were at one time made of cherry wood.

Have you noticed the holly trees? The leaves on the higher branches are almost round and smooth, those on the lower branches have prickles around their edges. I have been told that this is Nature's way of protecting the trunk from animals, who, when rubbing themselves against the tree, rub off the bark. Another old country saying!

We have now reached the gate into the farm yard. On our right is a sight that would have delighted William Wordsworth. A host of golden daffodils. A carpet of gold reaching as far as the eye can see. Sadly the farm house – built in the 1970s – although a fine house, is not built in the Sussex style.

On our left, a great barn with another close by, which houses the grain dryer, they seem to overpower the small farm yard. This type of barn is said to be of more service than the old flint and tile hung barns. Yet would any artist clamour to paint them as they did the old ones? Certainly they would not make such attractive pictures. This farm was not always as quiet as this, it once had a thriving dairy herd and at times there were at least

Like a land-locked whale . . . the old barn

six workers about the place. Now there is just one farm bailiff, with the help of contract workers in the busy seasons.

This part of the borstall is called the Street, although there are only six cottages in it.

These are a fine example of Victorian building in flint with tile hanging. The three cottages on the left were converted from stables. Those on the right replaced a small cottage that I have been told had a thatched roof. This work was carried out to the orders of C.H. Lane, whose house we shall be passing on the way home, I will tell you about him then.

The bungalow on the left was converted from the cow stalls and milking parlour. It looks very nice, but I would rather see the cows there and men busy about the place, as they were when Harold and Ron Thomas ran the farm for their mother. Dressed in their immaculate white hats and coats as they went about their tasks in the milking parlour. Regulations about the sale of milk stopped their milk round, now our milk comes from any old where.

By the telephone kiosk there was once a well, this was filled in during the 1930s. The filling sinks often and it has to be refilled. The picnic bench and table were placed there by Mr Guest who lives at Westmeston Lodge. For many years a large wooden granary stood there, almost blocking the view into Underhill Lane. It was removed when farming ceased here.

We will now cross the road and enter the churchyard by the lych gate. This gate has had a chequered life. Built by Mr Vigar, the carpenter for the Middleton estate at the turn of the century, it has been knocked down several times since the coming of the motor car. The names on the grave markers are interesting, as they record those who lived in the village or the neighbour-hood.

These on the right of the lych gate are of the Edwards family. Henry Edwards was for some years the parish clerk, another also Henry – was the bailiff for the Middleton estate. John Edwards was the village constable. Westmeston seems too small to have had a constable, yet it is recorded that for some years they had three. I wonder what their duties were! I under-stand that John Edwards was shot in the leg whilst chasing smugglers.

There are many stones to commemorate the Botting family. Farmers here for many generations, they farmed at Blackbrook and at Westmeston Place Farm. Near to them lay the Springates of Hayleigh Farm. Miss Springate played the harmonium for the church service here and at the Blackbrook church room, that stood on the edge of the common. This room was destroyed by fire on the night of October 14th 1962.

The two large table tombs to the south of the church are those of members of the Hodson family, silk merchants, who for a time lived at Westmeston Place Farm and were responsible for one of the enlargements to that house. They were related by marriage to the Lane family of Streat. Along the path to the east of the church, this grave once had iron railings around it. It is the resting place of Charles Heathcote Campion, sometime rector of this parish. He was thrown from his horse and killed whilst riding on the Downs. His body was found when his horse returned home without him. The accident happened near to the stile where we stopped to view the Weald. For many years an iron cross marked the spot. On the south side of this path, the tabernacle tomb of the Cripps family of Novington, and nearby the graves of the Stacey family of East Chiltington. Susanah Stacey is immortalised in the book *The Mistress of Stantons' Farm* written by Marcus Woodward.

Let us now enter the church. The interior always looks well cared for and is evidently well loved by those who worship here. Mr Murray, Priest in charge, Harold Rowling and Ivor Thomas, spent a lot of time in 1985 in cleaning the church, washing walls and ceiling, after repairs to the fabric had been carried out.

There are some very interesting features and memorials. The one that was most pleasing to me was stolen in 1985. This was a large lectern in the shape of a brass eagle. The thieves broke in through a small window in the vestry, although the lectern was very heavy and screwed to the floor, this did not deter them from taking it.

There was at one time a gallery where the musicians played the music for the services, this was removed during the restor-

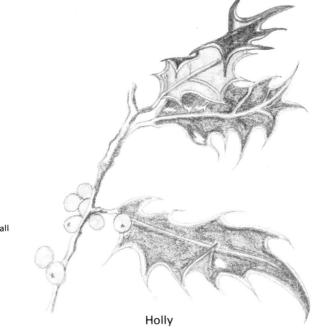

S. M. Hall

Holly

ations in 1868. At that time wall paintings were discovered and after a copy of them had been made, they were once again covered up, for it was thought that they were not of a high enough standard to be kept.

A list of past rectors is displayed on the south wall, although this list omits to mention the Puritan minister, appointed under the regime of Oliver Cromwell.

The south door was blocked up during the restorations, its position can be seen near to the children's corner.

We take the switching on of the electric lights for granted now, up to 1937 this church was lit by oil lamps, a messy task for the verger keeping them filled with paraffin oil, cleaning the glass chimneys and trimming the wicks.

A notice by the organ records the fact that the choir – trained by Mrs Grinstead – gained an honours certificate at Lewes Musical Festival in 1955.

One happening in this church is recorded in the documents appertaining to the Persecutions of the Society of Friends in Sussex: In the year 1657 John Pellatt, of Steyning, went into the steeplehouse of the parish of Westmeston, and the said John Pellatt was silent until after the priest had finished his sermon he then asked the priest questions touching on what the priest had said. The priest did not answer him, but called to the congregation to haul him into the churchyard, and there Joseph Studley, a Justice, who was present, committed him to prison. Three months later John was brought before the court at Lewes and as he would not admit to ill behaviour some persons present hauled him from the dock and tried to beat him. Richard Pratt and William Holbeam went to his assistance. For this they were also committed to the house of correction.

I wonder if we appreciate the religious freedom of today?

Outside again, the house to the north of the church is the Old Rectory; we saw its roof from the top of the Downs. The flowering trees look lovely against the dark flints of which the house is built. The grounds are private so I can not show you the corbells in the shape of animal heads which are above an angel who is depicted wearing a crown upon her head and holding in her hands what appears to be an heraldic shield.

This is the one house that does not appear to have a ghost, at least I have not heard of one. One man of note was born in the original House. The Reverend Edward Turner, one of the founder members of the Sussex Archaeological Trust, was born here in 1794. He was the third of the 13 children of the Reverend Richard Turner, who was curate here at that time.

We will leave the churchyard by the steps in the north west corner passing as we do so the tomb of the Izards, coal merchants of Brighton. I do not know why they are buried here or what connection they had with the village, they may have liked the quietness of this small churchyard after the bustle of Brighton.

Church Cottage is on our left, the date in the crest on the north wall denotes the time of an enlargement, carried out by C.H. Lane, and those are his initials. There seems to have been a dwelling here of some sort since before 1590, it was most likely the dairy and dairymaids' hovel. In 1597, John Batnor, the rector of Westmeston, was brought before the Archdeacons court to answer charges of various misdemeanours amongst these were the fact 'that there was no glass in the church windows' and that 'He did have his cattle served in the churchyard'.

We now cross the B2116 road and pass by Southbank Cottages, built about 1660, then passing Northbank Cottages, at the moment known as April Cottage and Culpepers, these cottages had their beginnings in 1638 and have Victorian extensions.

We will not take the path down into the road for a moment, but we will enter the field on this side of the road. This path would take us back into Ditchling, we do not wish to return there just yet. To the right of this path we can see Westmeston Place – the farm part of the name was dropped when it ceased to be the farm house. The oldest part of the house cannot be seen from this path. The part that can be seen was built in 1887 and added to in 1908/9.

The ghost that is said to haunt this house – and is reputed to have been seen by many people – is thought to be that of a monk, who at the time of the Reformation was caught by Henry VIII's men and killed whilst he was still carving a panel. Those persons who have seen the figure have all stated that he was standing before a half finished carving. This story being oft repeated, the panel was removed – at the request of the owners – in 1925 and now forms part of the reredos in Streat Church. The present owners tell me that they have not seen the figure, so maybe this has laid the ghost.

I have been told by previous owners of the house that there is a passage going underground from near to that oak door and that it leads to the vestry of the church; if true the passage must have taken a long time to dig.

I find that old barn to the south west of the house much more fascinating. Its history does not seem to have been recorded, but sit on the fence and have a rest and I will tell you what I think its story might have been.

Angels and Corbells on the south wall of the
Old Rectory, Westmeston.

The Old Barn

AS can be seen the barn blends well into the landscape and seems to squat like a land locked whale midst well tended lawns and flowering shrubs; these almost hide it from the casual glance, the barn's tile hung roof is supported by massive timbers, that were once long ago oak trees growing in the Weald.

One day the axe man came and felled those mighty oaks, then oxen – muscles straining under glossy coats – with chains attached dragged the stricken limbs and trunks to this secluded spot.

Here men, sinews stretched taught along wind-burnt arms, manoeuvred the great trunks upright to take the lesser limbs, that were used as cross members. Other timbers, roughly hewn, were pegged across them, the whole structure was then covered with a bracken thatch. Thus the barn was born, to shelter the meagre stocks of food that had to last those who laboured near through the winter months.

These men planted ash saplings to circle the barn, for when full grown not only would they serve as a wind break, but ash trees – thought those men – would guard their produce from the slivering snakes, and the bark distilled would relieve their aches and their pains. For these men of the Brotherhood of the College of St Michael, although they had embraced the new Christian religion had not entirely forgotten the habits of their forebears.

From the Downs around them, their herbalist gathered many types of herbs, these he laid upon the barn's floor to dry, and the pungent smell impregnated the oak posts.

After many years, the Brotherhood of St Michael were replaced by the brothers of St Pancras. These new monks, believing in the one God, cut down the ash trees; but did pagan thoughts still linger, for cutting the ash wood length ways into strips, they thus encased the barn in Ash. These new monks still collected and distilled the herbs, sheltered wayfarers, and helped the poor; many a man fleeing from the battlefield received treatment and succour beneath the barn's roof.

Sheep soon dominated the scene, and the shorn fleeces were stored in the barn; and there spinning wheels worked by the monk's capable hands spun the wool, and they then wove the yarn into habits for themselves and their bretheren.

In the reign of Henry VIII, the priories all over England were seized; this of course, included the little farmstead and the barn. The monks were turned out and became as the beggars that they themselves had succoured; but the barn stood firm.

The king's factor took over the running of the farm; the ash boarding around the barn – being riddled with damp and woodworm – was removed, and replaced with flints, the bracken thatch was replaced with tiles.

The barn was filled with the fruits of the serfs labours; for the king's and the factor's own use, the serfs and their families often went hungry. Still the mighty oaks stood firm, holding up the new roof proudly. Time moved on, civil war swept the country, houses and barns, even churches were pillaged and burnt, but the little barn, almost hidden in the lee of the Downs escaped unharmed.

The maypole, banished by Puritan law, was sheltered amongst the barn's highest beams, to reappear when a king once again reigned in England. Farming methods changed, the slow moving Oxen were replaced by horses; these would not only pull the plough and do other tasks around the farm, they also carried the farmer to hunt the scavenging fox.

In the dormant months many tasks were performed in the shelter of the barn's walls, amongst these the refurbishing of the waggons in the Sussex colours of red and blue.

Besides the duties about the farm, the waggons were used to take brides and grooms to their weddings at the little church, and when their lives had ended the waggons – decorated with evergreens– would carry them to their last resting place in the churchyard, in the shelter of the Downs.

At least once during the hunting season, the members of the hunt would drink their stirrup cup, whilst they stood chatting at the barn door, before starting the day's chase.

The inside of the barn was at some time divided into sections to house 60 cows, for instead of milkmaids going out into the fields to milk the cows, the cows were brought into the barn,

Boxing Day meet at Westmeston

and men took over the milking. The oak beams resounded to the lowing of the herd, intermingled with the soft burr of Sussex voices.

Time passed and, alas for the barn, the words hygiene and unhygienic were spoken by some who looked inside the doors, so the herd was disbanded; the barn once more became a store room.

Yet another war came and with it troops, armoured cars, and some noisy tanks, the house was requisitioned. Strange accents were heard as Canadian soldiers moved into the house. The barn's floor of chalk and earth, trodden solid by centuries of feet, was covered in concrete and the barn became their workshop. Tanks rumbled by, aircraft flew overhead and bombs were dropped. But still the mighty oaks stood firm.

The war over, the soldiers moved out and the builders moved in. The site was no longer a farm. The outbuildings were converted into dwellings for humans, flowering shrubs were planted and the grass lawns laid. The barn was sold with the other buildings and so was no longer part of Westmeston Place.

The barn was refurbished, white lines were painted upon its floor and the game of badminton was often played, accompanied by the joyful sound of young people laughing, the sounds echoed around the old oak beams. Each year for many years now, on the last Saturday in August, trestle tables are set up in the barn, people come from around the neighbourhood bringing with them the produce grown in their own gardens. The women bring the preserves that they have made in the long winter evenings. They set each exhibit with pride along the green baize covered tables; the ladies arrange their floral displays, then rearrange them with loving care; children emulate their parents in classes of their own. Then all leave the barn with a quiet confidence that their exhibit will catch the judge's eye and that they will receive a prize. At 2.30 pm, the doors of the barn will open to admit a steady stream of exhibitors and their friends, to exclaim over the prizes that they or a neighbour has been awarded. The barn seems alive with happiness.

The afternoon quickly passes and evening comes, the barn is cleared, some of the exhibits to be auctioned for a local charity. The prize winners receive their cups. The annual flower show is over; as the visitors leave someone is sure to say 'What a lovely old barn this is, I bet it could tell some tales.' The oak posts seem to stand straighter and taller. Yes, they could tell some tales, some happy, some sad, but the barn will keep its secrets, even its real age, which is something that I for one would really love to know.

Let us now climb back over the stile; have you noticed how well the footpaths are marked? This is the work of a small group of people who work voluntarily under the leadership of Harold Rowling and Reg Adsett, they are known as The MONDAY GANG. We cross the road and climb the steps – again the work of the same group of people – and we are in a small paddock. It was in this paddock, before that bungalow was built, that Westmeston fairs were held; one fair was always held on the feast of St Martin of Tours, and a cold one it must have been, for his feast day is November 11th. We skirt the northern hedgerow and pass behind the bungalow – built at the end of the 1914/18 war. We climb another stile, pass behind a flint wall and with the Old Rectory on our right hand side, we make our way through another paddock to a stile in its eastern

Haymaking in the Old Rectory paddock in 1928

hedge. It was in these fields that the men of the Aldershot Command held a summer camp in 1928.

This part of our stroll passes the northern boundary of Old Middleton. This house is thought to have had its beginnings in Tudor times. For some years it was divided into four dwellings, for some of the workers on the estate. When the estate was sold off in small parcels, these workers' homes were sold and converted into a gentleman's residence. Since that time it has been sold many times, each purchaser adding yet more rooms.

There is a ha–ha dividing the eastern front garden from the public bridlepath, it is this track that we turn into and we take the left hand fork, leaving the old barn on our right. Until 1985 there was a much larger barn standing near by, this was destroyed by fire. How very quiet it is now, but it was not always so; for the barn was once the carpenter's shop. The hunting hounds, and the gamekeeper's dogs were also kept here.

The poultry maid kept many hens, not only for the eggs, but also for table birds for the dinner parties, at the 'big house' when as many as a dozen would be needed for a sitting.

We have now reached the 'Big House' which we can see through the trees on our right. This is New Middleton House, although it is more often referred to as Middleton Manor, we saw its rooftop from the viewing place on the Downs.

The house was built in 1830 at the orders of Thomas Henry Lane, it was to this house that he brought his cousin, Jane Lambert, as his bride. They only had one child, Charles Henry Lane. Unhappily Thomas died in 1834, his widow Jane moved away with the young Henry – she later remarried and had a daughter. The house was let to tenants until Henry reached his majority, when he returned to New Middleton to live. Until that time the track on which we are walking was the only carriage entrance to the house. Henry had a driveway cut from the south west of the house to the Lewes road, where he also had a cottage built for a lodge keeper. Mrs Upton, and Mrs Hanper are among those who held this position.

Henry married his cousin Kathleen Lambert, they lived here until his death in 1908. Kathleen was some years younger than Henry. She remarried in 1918 to Henry Bothamley. Kathleen died in 1931.

There being no children of the marriage, the estate was sold. Henry is best remembered for the cottages he built for the estate workers, he had one other claim to fame: He was chairman of Westmeston Parish meeting for 11 years, but only attended one meeting in that time. The house remained in private hands until the outbreak of the 1939–45 war, when the house and grounds were requisitioned by the War Office and used as a holding camp for troops before they were sent overseas.

Later it was used as a prisoner of war camp, for German soldiers. After the war it was used for a time as an extension to Plumpton Agricultural College, then taken over by the East Sussex Health Authority for the training of young people with some mental problems. The flats to the north of the main building are for the use of these young students who are thought to have overcome their problems and are training to look after themselves in the outside world. It is difficult to imagine that up until 1939 there was a staff of 24 workers here. The estate was of 700 acres, now it is 25 acres. The original house had seven

Members of the Monday Gang in action

bedrooms, so one can see how greatly it has changed.

Before we continue our stroll, look back at that lovely view of the Downs and the V plantation. Henry Lane and his uncle, General Fitz Hugh – who lived at Streat Place – were responsible for its planting. This was done to commemorate the Jubilee of Queen Victoria in 1887. The planted area is 5,918 square yards. The number of trees planted was 2,997, these in 15 rows in each arm and the trees were planted 4ft apart, they are a mixture of pines, beech, birch and lime. The cost of the trees was just under £12. The first tree was planted in the apex by Mrs Lane, the tree on each side was planted by Mr Lane. The children from Westmeston and Streat schools were given the day off school; a picnic was arranged on the site and each child was encouraged to plant at least one tree.

Some of the trees did not survive, these were replaced in 1918. The plantation has almost overgrown, many trees are dead and it really could do with some attention.

Let us now continue our stroll northwards. On our left hand side of the track, a nice little drainage pond, with a brook running from it, under the path and away eastwards, the water to join with other waters to feed the River Ouse.

The pond is not as deep as ponds sometimes were, for they are not mudded as they used to be. What is mudded? When there was little water left in a pond, after a dry summer, the loose debris was raked off and removed, the surface was then reconsolidated. this used to be done about every five years.

Those water birds are moorhens, one can tell them from the other small water birds, the coots, moorhens wear a little red cap of feathers well down their foreheads, whilst the coots wear a little white cap of feathers, these look like a bald patch, from this we get the saying 'As bald as a coot'.

The students from Middleton built a wooden duck house on that fallen trunk that lies well out into the pond, they installed six pairs of duck, but it was not a success, the fox ate the ducks.

In the woods on our right, the Lanes had their horses buried when they died. Each horse had a stone engraved with its name, to mark its resting place; for a long time the stones lay buried in the undergrowth, they have now been removed to stand alongside the front drive of Middleton House.

The woodland to our left was cleared in the 1970s and was replanted with oaks with a nursery of pines, unfortunately the undergrowth threatens to strangle the new trees. This wood reaches from here to the B2116 road between Ditchling and Westmeston. We shall be skirting its northern boundary on the way home.

We have now reached a place where four bridleways cross, the one to our right takes one to Streat Lane, near to Sandpit Cottages. The path straight on passes Hayleigh Farm and on-wards through the Weald. This path is a spur of the Roman road that runs east/west and passes a few yards to the north of Hayleigh Farm.

I read in the Hundred Rolls that the Sheriff of Sussex was assaulted hereabouts, whilst he was collecting the taxes on behalf of the king. They obviously did not like the tax man then, as some people dislike him today.

I think some of the horsemen must have fled this way after the battle of Lewes, for on the days and nights of 22nd and 23rd of May, the sound of galloping horses can be heard coming

Old Middleton in 1916

from the south, then the sound recedes as they gallop away to the north, yet no horses can be seen.

We are taking the track to our left, this is called Whapple Way. This name has come to mean a bridleway, but it was not always so. A Whapple Way was a track upon which, besides horse riders, any cart or carriage with only two wheels was allowed to travel.

I do not think any vehicles would manage to get through here now without a great deal of difficulty, for even in dry weather the path is deeply rutted and waterlogged. We shall have to pick our way carefully for I wish to take you this way so that we can wait for dusk in Sedlow Wood.

Here we are, let us sit on that tree trunk, one that has fallen so conveniently near to the edge of the wood. Don't you think that is a wonderful sight? The sun is just sending out its last rays of fiery red rippling amongst the trees, and seeming to turn

New Middleton House in 1908

their fresh young leaves to bronze; to me it also seems to make the bark of the trees look like burnt orange peel.

The sweet-scented wild hyacinths and the wood anemones are closing their petals for the night. The woodland birds are ceasing their songs and all are settling down for the hours of darkness.

The slight spring breeze stills, the stag beetles, that have been chewing that rotten tree trunk, stop and curl up for the night, and look there is a tiny shrew eating the larvae of the stag beetles. A shrew is a tiny mouse-like creature which makes a continual chattering sound as if it is scolding.

The sun has finally put out its light, or as the ancients would have said 'Aurora has closed the gates to heaven and Apollo has gone to sleep'. All is cloaked in darkness, but our eyes will soon become accustomed to the dark, and there will be a full moon tonight, shining in the sky behind us.

Hear that rustling? The tawny owl in its tree top eyrie shakes out his feathers and with a loud TWOO, flies off to look for those small nocturnal creatures, like the shrews, who creep so unsuspectingly through the wood's undergrowth, for it is on these that he likes to feed his mate and his progeny.

The V plantation which dates from 1887

That heavy rustling, intermingled with loud grunts, is brock the badger off on a night's hunting; and there are his mate and cubs, they will play whilst awaiting his return, how sweet they look, tumbling like kittens in their play.

Badgers eat slugs and other small pests, although they are fond of frogs, and if hungry take eggs from the chicken runs.

Look at Reynard the Fox slinking by, he hardly makes a sound, he really looks like a lovable dog, what a pity that he is so destructive; all animals kill to eat, but he seems to kill for the pleasure and he leaves the corpses of chicken lying around uneaten, so we cannot forgive him.

The wood pigeon and the pheasants – feathers ruffled – perch on the higher branches of the trees, out of harm's way, for if there are no chicken or rabbits to be found Reynard will have them, if they perch too low.

Rabbits have a tough time, for if it is not man trying to kill them, and they escape the fox, the stoats will surely get them.

The earth is moving there, can you see it? That will be mole at work; day and night have no meaning to these underground workers. Mole is such a useful little creature, as he lives mostly on wire worms, although he does also eat earth worms. The wire worms do so much damage to the roots of the crops. I know that no one feels kindly towards moles when they tunnel under our well laid lawns, throwing up the soil into unsightly mounds. Moles are so small that it always amazes me when I read of gamekeeper's in olden times making the skins into waistcoats. Each coat would need so many skins, and what a lot of time would be spent in sewing them together.

Ah! That is what we have been waiting for; just listen to those few trembling notes of the nightingale, as he first practises before singing his song, a song so liquid, so clear, that he makes people like us stay from our beds just to hear him sing.

All Nature's creatures that move during the night seem to have stopped their activities to listen with us. Can any human voice compare in sweetness to the song of so small a bird as the nightingale? With the moon to light us, let us make our way westwards to the B2116 road, be warned if you should see a large black dog with a peculiar shaped front end, do not be afraid or try to stroke him, for it will be the ghost of the headless black dog that is said to haunt this area. The house on the other side of the road was built for Mr and Mrs Grahame Martin Turner in 1935/6 and they named the house after this unusual ghost. Grahame was a great cricket enthusiast and led a team of players, called 'The Black Dogs'. Their club tie was of white silk on which was the silhouette of a black dog, this dog naturally had its head slightly detached from its body.

We must now walk in single file down this road, for there is no footway, we do not want an accident like the one in 1928 when two young men were killed as they were walking up the hill, by the driver of a car coming down on the wrong side of the road.

We pass the southern end of Spatham Lane and stay on the right side of the road until we come to Shirley's. This estate is named for the Shirley family who once owned the land on which the houses are built. Their family home was at Wiston in West Sussex.

This road was at one time so narrow that the hedgerows on each side of the road met at the top, making in spring and summer a leafy tunnel.

All the houses along the south side of this road have been

built since the 1920s. The garage on our left was built by Mr Morley in 1929. The rough track beside the garage is the northern end of Nye Lane. We cross over the road at the southern end of East End Lane, but continue straight on, passing St Margaret's School, on our right. This school was built to replace the one near to the village church, which is now Ditchling's museum. Ditchling has had as many as 12 schools, two free schools, three boarding schools, the others were dame schools.

The field on which the school now stands, was once part of Gunn's Farm, and was one of the fields in which the troops from Brighton Barracks camped whilst on summer manoeuvres in this area. It was also used by the boys of Mr Branfoot's school for sports.

On the left we are passing the house known as Cleves, this was built at the beginning of the century, and was the house in which Edward Johnson the calligrapher lived and worked.

Our stroll is now at an end, we are back in the car park where we started this morning. As we part to go to our homes, the voices of the other birds are joining with that of the nightingale, the dawn is about to break, the cock will soon stretch his neck and crow, the dog released from sleep, will bark, both telling us that a new day is just beginning.

1938 — Ploughing on the Downs near Ditchling.

Westmeston Farm about 1908.